SMART ABOUT Art

HENRI MATISSE
DRAWING with SCISSORS

By Jane O'Connor
Illustrated by Jessie Hartland

Grosset & Dunlap • New York

For Barbara, an art lover
and a great friend—J.O'C.

For Sam, my favorite
little artist—J.H.

Cover image: *The Sadness of the King*, by Henri Matisse. 1952. Musee National d'Art Moderne, Paris, France/Giraudon/ Bridgeman Art Library. Page 15: Photograph copyright © 2001 by Olivier Rhee. All artwork by Henri Matisse copyright © 2001 Succession H. Matisse, Paris/Artists Rights Society (ARS), New York.

Library of Congress Cataloging-in-Publication Data

O'Connor, Jane, 1947–
    Henri Matisse : drawing with scissors / by Jane O'Connor ; illustrated by Jessie Hartland.
      p. cm — (Smart about art)
    Summary: Presents the life and work of Henri Matisse in the form of a child's school report.
    1. Matisse, Henri, 1869–1954—Juvenile literature. 2. Artists—France—Biography—Juvenile literature. [1. Matisse, Henri, 1869–1954. 2. Painting, French.] I. Hartland, Jessie, ill. II. Title. III. Series.
  N6853.M33 O28 2002
  736'.98'092—dc21   2001051275

ISBN 978-0-448-42519-1 (pbk.)   30 29

From the desk of

Ms. Brandt

Dear Class,

Our unit on famous artists is almost over. I hope that you enjoyed it as much as I did.

I am excited to read your reports. Here are some questions that you may want to think about:

- Why did you pick your artist?

- If you could ask your artist 3 questions, what would they be?

- Did you learn anything that really surprised you?

Good luck and have fun!

Ms. Brandt

Happy Birthday and Happy New Year

My artist, Henri Matisse, was born on New Year's Eve. So was I. That's why I chose him for my report. It is weird to have your birthday on December 31. I wonder if Henri Matisse got sick of people saying "Happy New Year" instead of "Happy Birthday." (I do!)

You say my name like this—
On-ree
Mah-teess

You say my name like this—
Kee-sha

Icarus from *Jazz*, by Henri Matisse. 1947. Pochoir plate. Scottish National Gallery of Modern Art, Edinburgh, UK/Bridgeman Art Library.

My grandfather sent me this card on my birthday. The picture is by Henri Matisse. I like the colors. They are so bright.

Henri and his mom

Henri was born here

FRANCE

Henri Matisse at age nineteen with his mother, Anna Héloïse Gérard Matisse. 1889. The Museum of Modern Art, New York. Copy Print © 2001 The Museum of Modern Art, New York.

LAW

Ethics

LAW

LAW

Henri was born in 1869. That is 125 years before me. He grew up in a small town in France. His parents ran a general store. His father wanted Henri to become a lawyer. Henri worked in a law office for a while but he was bored. He drew flowers on the law papers!

Then, when he was 20, Henri got very sick. He had to stay in bed for a long time. His mother gave him a set of paints to pass the time. That was it for Henri! From then on he knew he wanted to be a painter. His father said, "You'll starve!" But when he got better, Henri went to Paris anyway to become an artist.

This is one of the first paintings Henri did.

Still Life with Books and Candle, by Henri Matisse. 1890. Private collection/Bridgeman Art Library.

Henri painted this picture in 1890 when he was 20. You can tell exactly what everything is. The colors are dark, practically all browns and greens. This is the way art students were taught to paint.

The Snail, by Henri Matisse. 1953. Tate Gallery, London, Great Britain. Tate Gallery, London/Art Resource, NY

enri made this picture in 1953 when he was 83.
made from paper cutouts. I had no idea what
as supposed to be until I saw the title.
to guess what it is ... I wrote the answer
de down at the bottom of the page.) The
rs are so bright. Henri's art sure changed
from when he was a young artist.

Henri went to art school in Paris. He didn't like the teachers at his first school. So he went to a different art school. There he had a great teacher who told him to try using his imagination more.

Still Life with Kettle and Fruit, by Paul Cézanne. c.1890–94. Burstein Collection/Corbis.

Henri began to study what artists of the day, such as Claude Monet and Paul Cézanne, were doing. They were painting in a new way. They were using brighter colors and bigger brushstrokes.

This painting is by Paul Cézanne. Henri liked his paintings so much that he sold his wedding ring to buy one.

The Bottle of Schiedam, by Henri Matisse. 1896. Alexander Burkatowski/Corbis.

Henri's paintings started to change. He did this painting in 1896 when he was 26. It looks more like the Cézanne painting. It is a still life painting. That means it's a picture of things (like fruit and flowers) instead of being a picture of people or a landscape. Henri was starting to paint with loose brush-strokes and use brighter colors.

André   Henri   Maurice

Henri became friends with two young artists named André Derain and Maurice de Vlaminck. He and his friends started painting with weird colors. They didn't care about making things look real. Henri said that he wanted to make "colors sing without paying attention to rules and regulations."

In 1905 they had an art show together. People were shocked. They said that the pictures looked like "wild beasts" had painted them. Henri and his friends didn't mind. They started to call themselves the "Fauves." That's French for "wild beasts."

I drew some FAUVES the way the Fauves might.

Woman with the Hat, by Henri Matisse. 1905. Oil on canvas. San Francisco Museum of Modern Art. Bequest of Elise S. Haas. Photograph © San Francisco Museum of Modern Art.

Fauve rhymes with stove.

This is Henri's wife, Amelie. She is wearing a hat. But to me it looks like a heavy bowl of fruit is sitting on her head. The colors are strange. Her face is yellow and blue-green. Her neck is orange. Henri only painted like a Fauve for a few years. Then he decided he didn't like this style anymore.

Me in a heavy fruit salad hat

Here is Henri's family

The Family of the Artist, by Henri Matisse. 1911. Oil on canvas. Hermitage, St. Petersburg, Russia/Bridgeman Art Library.

Henri's wife, Amelie →

← daughter

his sons, Jean and Pierre ↑

I read that Henri sold very few paintings when he first became an artist. There wasn't always enough food for the family. For a while, the Matisses had to move back in with Henri's parents. I wonder if his dad said, "I told you so." But then some people started to buy Henri's paintings. By 1911, when he painted this picture, Henri was doing a lot better.

I like how Henri put so many different patterns in his pictures. The patterns look busy, but his family looks quiet and peaceful.

I found ▦ and many ⦀, dozens of ⁙, zillions of ⩘, big patterns, little patterns and even 🌿. Somehow it all goes together.

Here is me with my sister. We clash!

Quiet, dears

Are you awake?

Now I am dear.

Henri's art was the most important thing to him—even more important than his family. At dinner, Mrs. Matisse would ask the children to be quiet, because their father was thinking about his latest painting.

Henri also had a hard time sleeping because he worried so much about his art. He would wake up Amelie in the middle of the night and make her go for a long walk.

I think that Amelie was a very patient wi

By the time he was 40, Henri was famous. There were art shows featuring his work. People bought lots of his paintings. His family moved into a nice house outside Paris.

The Terrace, St. Tropez, by Henri Matisse. 1904. Oil on canvas. Isabella Stewart Gardner Museum, Boston, Massachusetts, USA/Bridgeman Art Library.

Henri painted this picture in St. Tropez in the south of France by the sea.

Henri also liked to travel. He especially liked hot, sunny places by the sea. Henri loved to paint the colors of the water and the flowers and trees. He was interested in how sunlight looked different in different countries.

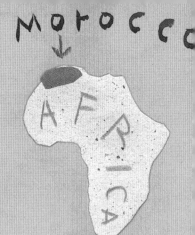

Henri first went to North Africa in 1905. In 1912 and 1913 Henri took two long trips to Morocco. He loved it. Staying in Africa changed how he painted. His pictures look calm and happy. The colors look like they are full of light.

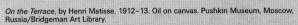

On the Terrace, by Henri Matisse. 1912–13. Oil on canvas. Pushkin Museum, Moscow, Russia/Bridgeman Art Library.

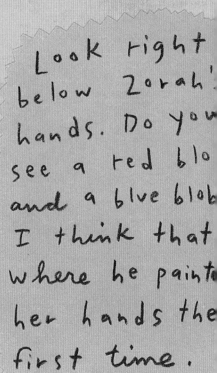

Look right below Zorah's hands. Do you see a red blo and a blue blob I think that where he paint her hands the first time.

This is a painting of a young girl named Zorah. She is Moroccan. You can tell that from her clothes. I read that Henri was hardly ever satisfied with what he did the first time around. He was always making changes and painting over things. I think that's what he did with Zorah's hands.

think all the shades of blue in this picture are beautiful. I counted five different blues. I bet if I saw the real painting, there would be even more. Henri painted lots of pictures with windows in them. You feel as if you are inside the room looking at what's outside.

Tangiers: View through a Window, by Henri Matisse. Pushkin Museum of Fine Arts, Moscow, Russia. Scala/Art Resource, NY.

I drew this picture looking out my bedroom window. That's my friend Natalie waving. She lives across the street.

As Henri got famous, people asked him to do pictures especially for them. This is called a commission. A rich business-man named Sergei Shchukin loved Henri's art. He bought lots of Henri's paintings. In 1910 Mr. Shchukin asked Henri to do a big painting for his mansion. He wanted a picture of dancers.

My Matisse! They're here!

To: Mr. Shchukin
France

FRAGILE

Dance II, by Henri Matisse. 1910. Oil on canvas. Hermitage, St. Petersburg, Russia/Giraudon/Bridgeman Art Library.

This is the painting that Henri did. Mr. Shchukin wasn't so sure that he wanted naked dancers in his front hall. Maybe he had wanted ballerinas in tutus. But he took the painting anyway.

The Dance (Merion Dance Mural), by Henri Matisse. 1932–33. Oil on canvas. The Barnes Foundation, Merion, Pennsylvania, USA/Bridgeman Art Library.

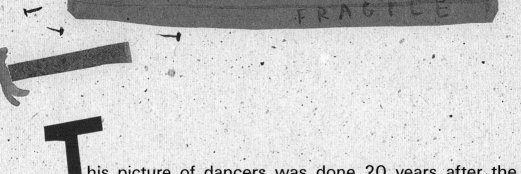

This picture of dancers was done 20 years after the other painting of dancers. Henri was 60. The painting is a strange shape because it was supposed to fit in the top of a wall with curved arches that was in an art gallery near Philadelphia. Henri made it look like some of the dancers are leaping right out of the painting. Before he started to paint, Henri cut out paper shapes of the dancers to figure out how he wanted them arranged. He moved the cutout pieces around until everything looked just right to him.

This painting is more than 40 feet long.

After he finished the painting, Henri found out that someone had sent him the wrong measurements. Henri's picture was too small! He had to start all over again! The whole thing took three years. Henri was exhausted. It was bad for his health and bad for his family. Henri and Amelie no longer lived together.

As he got older, Henri was often sick. He now lived in southern France by the sea where the weather was mild and sunny. In 1941 Henri had to have a big operation. He had cancer. He was 71 and nearly died. Henri had to stay in bed for a long time, but he felt very lucky to be alive. He said, "Every day that dawns is a gift to me."

Henri Matisse working on paper cutout. Bettmann/Corbis.

Henri had trouble painting because he couldn't stand up for long periods of time. So he cut out paper shapes, lots and lots and lots of them. He called it "drawing with scissors."

MAKING CUTOUTS

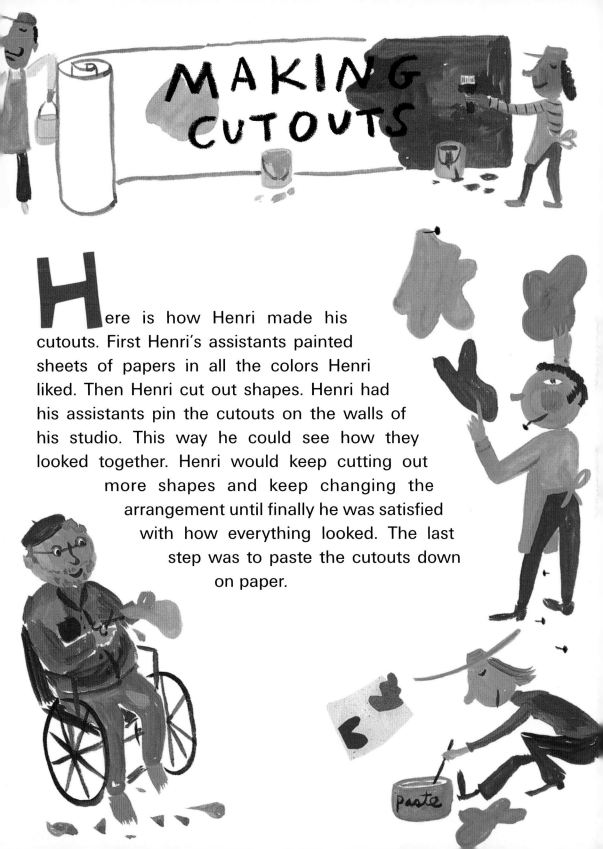

Here is how Henri made his cutouts. First Henri's assistants painted sheets of papers in all the colors Henri liked. Then Henri cut out shapes. Henri had his assistants pin the cutouts on the walls of his studio. This way he could see how they looked together. Henri would keep cutting out more shapes and keep changing the arrangement until finally he was satisfied with how everything looked. The last step was to paste the cutouts down on paper.

paste

La Gerbe (The Sheaf), by Henri Matisse. 1953. Gouache on paper, cut and pasted on paper, mounted on canvas. Collection of the University of California, Los Angeles. Gift of Mr. and Mrs. Sidney F. Brody.

HM 53

I have a leaf collection. I love their shapes and colors. I made some cutout leaves too. Cutting is hard work. Your hands get tired. I read that Henri played the violin for two hours every day. He loved music, but he also did it to give his hands a workout! Henri's picture looks simple, but now I know it wasn't. Like everything Henri did, it took lots of work.

When he was 73, Henri made 20 cutout pictures for a book that he wrote, called *Jazz*. The picture that my grandpa sent me on my birthday was in the book. I saw a copy of the book at the library. The words are all in Henri's own handwriting. They're in French. The book is not about jazz music at all. It's about Henri's feelings about being an artist.

Here is a page from JAZZ.

Circus, Plate II from *Jazz,* by Henri Matisse. Paris, E. Tériade, 1947. Pochoir, printed in color, page: 16 5/8 x 25 5/8". The Museum of Modern Art, New York. The Louis E. Stern Collection. Photograph © 2001 The Museum of

When he was 80 years old, Henri worked on something he had never done before. It wasn't a painting or a book or paper cutouts. It was a whole little church! It was going to be built in France, not far from where he lived.

Henri Matisse chatting with priest. Chapelle du Rosaire, Vence, France, 1951. © Bettmann/Corbis.

This is what the outside looks like.

The Altar, Saint Dominique and the Tree of Life (stained glass window), by Henri Matisse. Chapelle du Rosaire, Vence, France, 1950–51. Photo: H. del Olmo. Réunion de Musées Nationaux/Art Resource, NY.

Henri decided what everything would look like. He designed the building. He made the designs for the stained-glass windows; he did the drawings on the walls; he even designed the clothes for the priests. He did it because he was a good friend of one of the nuns. She had been his nurse when he was very sick. This was Henri's way of saying thank you.

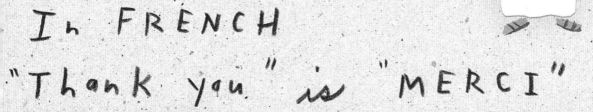

In FRENCH "Thank you" is "MERCI"

H MATISSE 52

Henri was old and sick, but he kept on working. His daughter said that Henri worked right up to the day he died. People say that some of his last cutout pictures are his greatest.

Henri died on November 5, 1954. He was almost 85 years old. He had been an artist for more than 60 years. He made paintings, sculptures, drawings, costumes for ballets, cutouts, books and even stained-glass windows. Henri was hardly ever happy with his art. But he hoped that it made other people feel happy. It does!

merci, Henri.

If I met Henri I would ask him
1) Why did you call your book *Jazz*? (Do you like jazz?)
2) Did you listen to music while you painted?
3) Did you have fun being a Fauve?

*Merci, Keesia, for your report. It is great. It is too bad that Henri was not a happier person, because his art certainly makes people feel happy. Did you know that he was friends with Pablo Picasso? Henri and Picasso are considered the two greatest artists of the 20th century.

Ms. Brandt